Scotland

Other books by Gary Greenberg

The Book of Woe:
The DSM and the Unmaking of Psychiatry

Manufacturing Depression:
The Secret History of a Modern Disease

The Noble Lie:
When Scientists Give the Right Answers
for the Wrong Reasons

Scotland

Gary Greenberg

New London Librarium

Scotland

Published by
New London Librarium
P.O. Box 284
Hanover, CT 06350
NLLibrarium.com

First Edition
Printed in the United States of America

ISBN-13: 978-0-9905899-2-1
ISBN-10: 0990589927

10 9 8 7 6 5 4 3 2

Gary Greenberg

Scotland

When my then wife and I moved to Scotland, the tiny Connecticut town where I have lived for the past thirty years, we awoke on our first Sunday morning to find a batter-filled bowl covered in Saran wrap on our front porch. There was a note attached. It explained that the sourdough in the bowl, when mixed with flour and other ingredients and baked, would make a Welcome Cake. And, it continued, if we set aside some of the batter, we would be able to pass it along to our children (and presumably to any new arrivals we might want to welcome). The cake yielded by the recipe was crusty and, as might be expected, a little sour.

The note was unsigned, and we never did find out which of the thousand people then living here left us the gift. We thought the anonymity was odd, and vaguely creepy, but, as I was soon to discover, we're not big on introductions around here. Run into someone you know because he has laid bricks for you or because you've drilled with him on Monday nights at the firehouse, and if either or both of you have your wife in tow, you're not going to do the howdy-dos. Later, you will explain to your wife who that guy was. You will say, "Oh, he's the assistant fire chief." Or you will say, "He works for the guy who dug our septic system." You could live here thirty years and not know the name of the wife.

It's not only the famous Yankee reticence that explains this. It's also the fact that introductions are hardly necessary when you've known everyone all your life, when you've heard about someone long before you've met him, when everyone has a brother married to a cousin of the niece of the man in front of you, when you've all gone to the same two- or three-room schoolhouse, when you've cut each other's hay and driven each other's trucks and put out each other's fires, and when, unless you join the army or have the traveling bug or meet a man whose job takes you away, you may well be born, live, die, and be buried in town.

If you happen to have been Charles Perry, a tall, lantern-jawed man who wore a black and red checkered jacket even on the warmest days, you can do all that within the space of less than a mile. Until well into his eighties, Charles tended the lawn at the grange hall next to my house. He had grown up in the gray center-chimney colonial across the road from our 1840 Cape Cod, moved into the tidy house two doors down when he got married, and lived there until he died, at which time he was buried in the cemetery just down the road. Along with his brother John, Charles worked as a carpenter, mostly on the homes right here in town. Their father, Clarence, also a carpenter, was town clerk and treasurer, jobs his wife Honor eventually took over. The land records were kept in their home until a proper vault was built in the Town Hall on the other side of the road. John Perry settled in a white 18th-century Cape two doors north of Charles's house and just adjacent to a slightly

less old beige gambrel-roofed home. Both houses
are set back a couple hundred feet from Devotion
Road. They sit side by side atop a knoll, a pair of
dowager sisters, their skirts spilling out toward the
road. Just north of the white house is Perry Motors,
housed in a converted carriage barn, and one of the
three storefronts that comprise the village business
district. Russell Perry, John's son, who grew up in
the white house and now lives in the beige house,
has been running the garage since 1958, when his
uncle Raymond, who started it, keeled over dead.
Russell was 19 years old. He's 75 now, and still
breaking loose rusted bolts with forearms like
Popeye's. He's busy, but never too busy to come
out from under a car, wipe his hands on a rag and
tell a story about something that happened in town
thirty years ago or yesterday. Russell already owns
his plot in the Scotland cemetery.

Perry Motors, the white Congregational
Church, a Catholic chapel, the general store, the
Pins and Needles sewing shop (housed in the old
firehouse), the Town Hall with its green shutters
and the belfry left over from the days when it was
the elementary school, the Perry houses, and my
old house and five or six others—these all flank

the green, a tree-lined parklet with a gazebo at its center. In the winter, when icicle lights hang from the gazebo and reflect off the snow, and the village houses shine candles in their windows, I can't help but be reminded of Currier and Ives, although sometimes the scene puts me in mind of Conestoga wagons circled around a fire.

A few years before I moved to town, the Ku Klux Klan staged a rally in Scotland. Writing for the *Harvard Crimson*, Bill McKibben reported that it was the first Klan rally in New England since the turn of the century. McKibben wasn't the only journalist in attendance; the rally made the CBS evening news, and a small army of reporters and hundreds of protestors followed the thirty or so hooded Klansmen from the town green, down Devotion Road, passing the house I would later move into, then left onto Cemetery Road, up the hill to Teeny Rood's farm. Skirmishes broke out along the way, but once the Klansmen had set up camp in Teeny's meadow, they could give their speeches unmolested. When night fell, they burned the 20-foot cross they'd erected for the occasion. People were still talking about the Klan rally when I moved in, and although Teeny is dead and his house has burned to the ground, they're still talking about it today.

When Teeny had a stroke in the early '90s I was one of the volunteer firemen who laid him on a gurney and wheeled him out of his house, around the chimney that had crumbled to the ground years before, and into the ambulance. I had the position next to his head. He looked up at me with panic-widened eyes. Driving him to the hospital in Willimantic, a small mill city ten miles away, I thought about how emergency had obliterated a natural enmity, and how community is a response to the prolonged emergency of being alive.

The fact that I was driving the ambulance; that an outsider, a wiry, brain-working Jew no less, had shown up one night at the firehouse and been granted membership, although tentatively and maybe even grudgingly, by the beefy farmers and mechanics; that over the previous eight years or so they had (after asking to see my commercial driver's license) overcome their suspicions enough to put me behind the wheel of their fire trucks and farm equipment; that they had elected me to public office; that they seemed to listen when I spoke at town meetings and to respect me, to confide their psychological troubles to me, and even, occasionally, to like me—all of this made me feel grateful. It made me wonder if Thomas Hobbes deserved his reputation as a hardass: useful as it is, there's also something noble and beautiful about working together to make life less nasty, brutish, and short. And maybe even impractical: it might have been a lot easier on everyone to just let Teeny die on the floor of his home.

Not that I have ever been lost enough in the haze of nostalgia to think that bigotry or any of the other pathologies of insularity died with Teeny. At the firehouse after a car wreck or brush fire, leaning on the bed of a pickup truck in front of the post office, standing in the pit of a milking parlor at 4:30 on a winter morning with steam rising off the splashing cows, their piss splashing my face, washing shit off their udders and tweezing their teats into the hydra-headed milker, I've heard men who have never been more than fifty miles from home go on about the lazy Hispanics in "Willi-Rico" and their pimped-out Toyotas, about people on welfare whose kids get expensive special services in school, and increasingly—as the years went by and the population swelled above 1,500 and each successive election revealed an increasingly conservative electorate—about the "Goddamn federal government," as one man put it when he discovered the post office locked up for lunch at 2 p.m. and kicked its door for emphasis. Occasionally, someone forgets himself long enough to brag about having "Jewed down" a car salesman. Sometimes he will apologize to me. I shrug, as if to say no big deal.

Which it isn't, or at least it isn't shocking. I figure casual bigotry is universal, and I appreciate their apologies the same way I appreciate an apology for a long, loud, smelly fart. Not only that, but the apologies signify that they care about me in some small way. The regrets, at least as much as the slur, signify our differences; and I, the descendant of refugees, a onetime cabin-dwelling hermit, a heretic in my profession, weaned on alienation and yearning to belong somewhere—I wanted a home, and I thought I'd found one, and I didn't want too much attention drawn to anything that so marked me as an outsider.

Still, I am aware that in all the talk about the Klan rally, I've never heard anyone despise the Klan the way they despise Dan Rather or the ACLU or the people who came to protest. I know that only a few millimeters beneath the surface comity is a flinty bedrock of intolerance and ignorance and xenophobia, and, ready to spring from its underground reservoirs, no small measure of murderous hatred. All along, that is to say, I've known that the people of my little town are fully capable of a lynching, symbolic if not corporeal. I just never imagined that the person they would lynch would be me.

Perhaps I should have known this too. Surely I know what Plato and Burke and Jefferson knew: that it doesn't take much for democracy to teeter over into mob rule. I'd harnessed that power more than once—about ten years ago, for instance, when I rose from my seat at a town meeting to bring the assembly's attention to certain fiscal irregularities that cast suspicions of petty till-tapping on the assistant town clerk and the first selectman (the executive elected to run the town according to the will of the town meeting). I tried to sidestep the question of the women's culpability and draw attention to the real problem, as I saw it: that the town was still running its business the way it did when Honor and Clarence Perry kept the books in their parlor. The town meeting voted to adopt certain measures I proposed to tighten up the ship, and the women survived—one is now the town clerk, the other the administrative assistant to the first selectman, a job she seems to love. I think they have forgiven me, but no one has forgotten that night. Some people still think of them as a pair of thieves and take their continued presence at Town Hall as an affront.

I didn't mean for that fight to get personal, but when it came to my battle with the chairman of the zoning commission, I did. Guy was a swaggering Italian-American whose family had settled in Scotland in the early 1900s and became dairy and chicken farmers. His father was the brother of a man who, along with another young Italian man, had wooed identical twin girls who were nannies to a family that lived here in the summers. The resulting marriages had created a large clan of farmers and truckers and mechanics and loggers. Guy had taken over his father's chicken business and owned coops housing more than a quarter-million birds. He didn't look the part. He drove a Jaguar, flaunted his sizable belly, smoked expensive cigars, and wore gaudy rings, a gold chain around his neck, and a pointy, jet-black Van Dyke. Without any apparent irony, he dismissed people with whom he disagreed by brushing the back of his hand under his chin.

Zoning commissions are easy to vilify. They stand for all the ways that government treads on us, limiting our deeply held sense that we are free to do what we want with what we own. They tell people that they have to build their houses here, that they can't operate their business there, that they have to hire an engineer and maybe a lawyer and get the signatures of functionaries and pay a fee in order to get the government's permission to give a building lot to their children. On the other hand, zoning boards also function to etch the status quo into the stone of regulations, a power that liberty-minded people are glad to seize when it suits them, much as the staunchest Tea Partier is pleased to drive on the interstate, cash his Social Security check, and present his Medicare card at his doctor's office.

With Guy at the helm, Scotland's zoning board did as much as possible to prevent change while preserving the liberties of those who already had them. Rickety garage apartments, unauthorized swimming pools, rogue repair shops, and storage yards that had sprung up over time and become part of the landscape—these were all ignored. Every once in a while the commission did enforce its regulations, but mostly, or so the people involved complained, against outsiders or people unrelated to Guy by blood, marriage, or long twining friendships. Guy used his don's contempt to dispense with the few objections anyone bothered to raise, and people grew bitter and whispered their suspicions. Still, every six years, like clockwork, they re-elected him—mostly because no one ever bothered to run against him. But then one day in 1998 word got out that Guy announced he was planning to build a 265-foot cell tower where his coops, which had burned down ten years before, once stood—less than a half-mile from the town green. The tower would interrupt the view of the valley in which the village was nestled, a panorama of steeple and fields and hills in the distance that had remained unchanged for hundreds of years. Partly to prevent just such an occurrence, the zoning laws had made such a structure too tall by an order of magnitude—unless it was a television aerial for a private residence, upon which there were no height limits. "I am going to get great reception," Guy said.

Soon after construction began, the official who had signed the permits for the tower quit. The town hired a new zoning agent named Carl. An outsider, he rode into town in a white Ford pickup, and like a U.S. Marshal in a western, vowed to clean up the mess he had discovered. He went after the various illegal businesses, and, noting that Guy's tower had not been completed, told him his building permits had expired. To finish it, Carl said, Guy was going to have to apply all over again. And he intended to hold Guy to the rules; if he couldn't qualify for the permit, he'd have to dismantle the tower. Guy fired Carl, and when it turned out that only the board of selectmen could do that (and they wouldn't), he proposed instead to change the zoning regulations to eliminate the agent position and appoint himself as the enforcement agent. It was a move opposed by the town lawyer and the board of selectmen, but not by the zoning commission, and it was their game. To win it, however, they would have to hold a public hearing.

It cost me $250 in postage to photocopy and mail a letter to every household in Scotland. The town clerk, sympathetic to the cause, provided me with voter rolls for addresses, and she and a couple of others stuffed the envelopes after hours at Town Hall. The letter explained the cell tower and the scofflaws and the planned ouster of Carl, called it a "cynical attempt" to circumvent the will of the citizens, and urged them to turn out for the hearing. People already knew about all of this, of course, but the letter helped to galvanize them, and a couple of hundred showed up—more, by some accounts, than any meeting in recent history, even the ones about the Klan. Guy didn't help himself much. As the town attorney had refused to attend, he hired a bullet-headed lawyer who wore a suit with shoulder pads. He kept leaning over and whispering in his ear as citizen after citizen stood up and repeated in his or her own words the charges my letter (and my speech at the meeting) had lodged: abuse of power, disrespect for the rule of law, favoritism. Guy managed to keep his hand from under his chin, but he was combative and abrupt and held everyone to a strict three-minute time limit, restricting them to only one turn each, and only in the order in which they had signed up at the beginning of the night. Soon, however, his control over the crowd foundered. People spoke out of turn, and repeatedly, and with increasing vituperation that inspired increasingly raucous applause and catcalls, until Guy looked like a boxer pummeled to the ropes, his hands hanging down to his sides. At the stroke of 10 o'clock, as he had promised to do, he closed the hearing. I had the last word of the evening. "I'm proud of all of us," I said. "Ain't democracy great?" We left the meeting together, shaking hands and slapping backs, drunk on democracy and swollen with self-righteousness.

Within a month of that meeting, after some shrewd political and legal maneuvering, Guy was gone and the town had a new zoning commission with a new chairman: me.

It's not really fair to Guy or to Scotland, not to mention to African-Americans (other than Clarence Thomas), to call this a lynching. It's also not fair to the South; New England has its own long history of public furies, the expulsions, scarlet letters, and confinements to the village stocks that you read about in history books. Occasionally, as alleged witches and heretics and adulterers have found out, true violence has broken through. Either way, I was thinking of Jefferson more than Hawthorne or Anne Hutchinson when we took down Guy—probably because it hadn't happened to me yet.

In my thirty years in Scotland, I've divorced, remarried, raised a son, moved out of the village and into a house I built at the edge of a state forest. I have made the transition from newcomer to old-timer, if not exactly an honorary native. I know hundreds of my fellow townspeople. Most people have some vague idea of what I do, that I am a head doctor of some kind, but very few know I am also a writer (although I believe the library stocks my books). People ask for permission to hunt on our land. I borrow tools and crack jokes at which other men laugh. I go to breakfast many Saturdays with men who have lived here all their lives. I don't listen to the country music station or dip snuff (although my son does both), but I wave to the town road crew and the school bus drivers and the farmers and they wave back. I often fail to introduce my wife. When the eagles soar out of the early morning fog on the Shetucket River or when the winter sun glints off the snow, I feel lucky to live here. Town-proud, I stop to clear branches that fall in the middle of the street, call farmers when their cows are wandering in the road, tell the town crew when a culvert is clogged. I have come to love this little town the same way you love a wife or an old friend—unconditionally, and sometimes despite yourself, because they have become a part of you. And I have come to believe that the town returns the feeling.

I've been zoning chair for nearly half my time here. We've passed regulations that made it possible for all the illegal businesses to come in out of the cold and for newcomers to feel like they aren't at a disadvantage. We've compelled would-be developers to set aside 40 percent of their land as permanent open space. We've outlawed dog kennels and made it easier to have a beauty shop in your home. We've disappointed some people, angered others, and occasionally earned the gratitude of an aggrieved neighbor. Thanks to the terrible economy and our distance from the interstate, we've been spared high-stakes fights over housing developments—feared largely because they bring in schoolchildren, who are terribly expensive to educate; there hasn't been a major subdivision here in decades. Repeated rumors of a Dunkin' Donuts replacing the general store have proved to be exaggerated, but in the meantime we've enacted regulations that might make such an enterprise difficult to achieve.

Scotland

The commission, in short, has worked hard to prevent change from overwhelming whatever it is that people have gotten used to. We meet once a month, ten people who represent what passes for diversity in this white, Christian, unaffluent town: a young dreadlocked single mother and farmer, a professor from the local community college, a couple of retirees, an inventor, a salesman, a contractor, a descendant of the founding family of the town, and, of course, a Perry, grandnephew of Clarence and Honor. We all have a vague idea of one another's politics, but we steer clear of them and somehow manage to achieve consensus on nearly every decision we make. Sometimes I imagine this is exactly what Jefferson had in mind: yeoman-legislators volunteering to put aside difference and ideology and self-interest for the greater good, zoning our way to a peaceable kingdom.

The rage always seethes, however: a little tremor in the voice or flush in the cheek of a commissioner as we debate how many dogs make a kennel or how far a garbage bin should be from a property line, and even more from our usually scant audiences, especially when people are asking our permission for something they think is their God-given right, or trying to stop something they think is an obvious evil. A man denied a permit to build a garage threatened one night to come to the next meeting packing his pistol. A years-long fight with a trucker—whose belief that the fifty-dollar permit he needed to store his trucks on his property was an unacceptable infringement upon his liberty had the support of many residents—resulted in a federal discrimination lawsuit against me. After one particularly contentious encounter with him, our power went out in the middle of the night. Later, still before dawn, I heard the utility company trucks at the bottom of my driveway and went down to investigate. "Got any enemies?" the lineman asked. He shined his flashlight on the puddle of oil at the base of the pole and then up at the bullet hole in the ruined transformer out of which it had leaked.

It's at times like this that I think we should take a line from Sartre and modify it for our slogan. It would be written on the blackboard hanging in the old classroom on the second floor of Town Hall in which we meet. *L'enfer, c'est les autres*, it would say, *en particulier les voisins.*[*]

---

[*]   Hell is other people, especially neighbors.

Scotland

In November 2013, a man named Peter called me on behalf of Reliance House, a nonprofit organization in a nearby city that delivers services to disabled people. Three of their clients had expressed a desire to move out of their current homes and in with each other, and the nonprofit had their eyes on a house in Scotland, a ranch hard by the state highway that had in the recent past burned, been rebuilt, undergone foreclosure, and sat for years as its value plummeted. The reason he was calling, Peter explained, was that these three "developmentally disabled" men were also registered sex offenders. Did Scotland have any zoning regulations that would forbid Reliance House from buying the house and renting it to these men?

The answer, according to our lawyer, was a little complicated. Per our regulations, a single-family home could be occupied only by a family, which was in turn defined as a "group of people related by blood or marriage." Clearly, the proposed arrangement violated this regulation. But so did many households in town, including my own (our son is adopted) and all the other people living together without benefit of marriage or blood relation. The definition, our lawyer said, was probably illegal, but more to the point, we couldn't exactly start enforcing it now, especially not against people protected by the Americans with Disabilities Act. To avoid civil rights prosecution, we had to treat Reliance House exactly as we would treat any other homeowner who wanted to rent out his house to a group of unrelated people, which meant that Reliance House was free to do what it wanted without any consultation with the zoning board.

A few days after I relayed this news to Peter, he called back. "They say Scotland is a pretty rough place," he said. He'd heard about the Klan rally, and wondered what would happen if people heard that sex offenders had moved to town.

I told him that that everyone here knows everything about everyone else and that privacy was about people choosing not to tell you they knew. In this case, I assured him, Yankee reticence would not prevail. "You can expect a real shit storm," I said.

At our next meeting, I told the commission about the problem in our regulation about family. I pointed out that unless we wanted to go around giving blood tests, demanding marriage licenses, and ordering people to cease and desist from living together, we could not enforce that law, and that this was probably a good thing. So, I suggested, we should adopt a new definition of family.

Over the next few months, we settled on a regulation that allowed people related by blood, marriage, adoption, or foster arrangements, or up to five unrelated people to live together. As we wrapped up the discussion, Larry, a bearded retiree, balked. "Do we have to call this 'family'?" he asked. "I have a problem with the zoning board redefining family." Larry never said exactly what the problem was, but I could guess. He drives the Christian Fellowship's church bus. He's also a pragmatist. He knew he couldn't stop the state from legalizing gay marriage or the federal government from recognizing it. For the Feds or the state to redefine family was one thing. But for the town in which he had grown up and lived all his years, just behind the house where his parents had lived and up the road from his daughter and grandchildren, that was woven as tightly into his identity as his craggy face or his rusty Dodge truck or his habit of clearing his throat—for his town, *his town*, to ratify the gay agenda, and with his assent if not his agreement: I figured this was not what he wanted to do.

I told him I would have the lawyer look into whether it was possible to call the group of people who live in a single-family dwelling something other than a family. The lawyer's answer was that of course we could do that—if we wanted to pay the legal fees to revamp our regulations to make sure that the word was purged and replaced with a suitable substitute and that the substitute wouldn't create unforeseen problems. In other words, given the fiscal realities of small-town New England, and the unlikelihood that the town meeting would be pleased to expend funds on an ideological adventure that put us on the cutting edge of land-use law, the answer was no.

Larry seemed satisfied, if not happy, when I delivered the news at the next month's meeting, and he joined the rest of us in voting to bring the new definition of family to the town for a hearing.

Not too long after, in late March, I got another call from Peter. He wanted me to know Reliance House had decided to go ahead and buy the house, and that the closing was imminent. I wished him luck when the news came out. A few days later, I got an email from the town clerk. "While I was on vacation last week," she wrote, "a strange conveyance took place." The strangeness amounted to this: the owner was a real estate company no one had heard of, the person who had recorded the deed had also purchased a set of zoning regulations, and the price paid for the home—$188,000—"was pretty high for this market." Even as she was typing this email, she continued, her assistant was checking the sex-offender list (she didn't say why) and discovering that it included a man who had listed the newly purchased home as his address. And, what was more, while this was going on, a "very concerned resident" was in her office, having caught wind that "high-risk sex offenders" were moving into town. "I have not informed her of any of this information because she is very upset and I didn't want to add to her fear." She told me to expect a call from the very upset woman.

I called her first and arranged to meet with her at Town Hall that same afternoon. She arrived in her pickup truck, a short 40ish woman in blue jeans with long curly dishwater-blond hair. She was wearing white earbuds, which she kept in while we talked. I couldn't tell if they were playing anything.

She told me she had been the victim of a sexual assault, which she described to me in horrific detail and with great emotion. I let her finish, told her how sorry I was that this had happened to her, and tried to explain that, unfortunately for her, the zoning board had no jurisdiction over the arrangement. I added that I was pretty sure that these men were not kidnappers, like the men who had assaulted her. I explained that even though these residents were no longer under the control of the state, their disabilities were severe enough to require round-the-clock monitoring by Reliance House's staff, so we were safer from them than from the three other registered sex offenders who, according to the registry, were already in town. I told her that we were in the process of rewriting our definition of who could live together in a house, that a public hearing was being held in the next month, and that this might be a forum to discuss whether situations like this could be prevented in the future.

"I see you've made up your mind already," she said. She was near tears. "This is what I moved to the country to get away from!" she said. "These people don't belong here. They belong in Norwich!" she added, referring to a grimy city a dozen miles down the road that had once housed a large state mental institution, and where Reliance House is headquartered. I explained that because Reliance House had the right to own the house and rent it to whomever they pleased, there was nothing to have made up my mind about, and I sympathized again with the position that this put her in. I pointed out that she herself was renting out part of her house to a tenant, and that there was nothing in the zoning regulations to stop that either. "But he's not a sex offender," she said. Shortly later, she left, unplaced.

Downstairs, the town clerk was still looking into the matter. "Btw there doesn't seem to be any discussion had in the minutes" about the sex-offender house, she emailed. "It should have been an open discussion for towns people to know about?" I wasn't sure if she was asking or telling, so I told her that people approach me all the time with ideas, some more crackbrained than others, wanting to know if they are compliant, and that until they formally approach the zoning commission, or (if they don't need to do that) until they carry out their plans, I'm just as in the dark as anyone else. I explained that I found out that Reliance House had gone through with their plans just a couple of days before she did. I repeated all this information that night when I called another man named Peter, this one a farrier. He is lanky and thickly bearded, with large hands and bulging eyes. Without any makeup, he could play Ichabod Crane in a local production of *Sleepy Hollow*.

I've known Pete for many years. Our sons are in school together, I've been to parties at his house, and we've talked enough about matters other than trucks and horses to know that we are not cut from the same political cloth. But Pete is forceful and charismatic and articulate, and I figured he would have the ear of the citizens who, I was sure, were already in a stir, and might be able to help to calm them down with the facts about the situation, which I relayed to him. When I told him the residents were developmentally disabled, he asked me, in his thick Boston accent, what that meant. "I don't know. They can't say more than that. HIPAA, you know"

"Yeah, HIPAA."

"But I think it might mean that they are severely autistic. And they are supervised round-the-clock. One aide for each man, line-of-sight coverage."

"And who pays for that?" he wanted to know. He told me his theory about how this was just the government trying to wash its hands by contracting with a private agency, or maybe it was the private agency trying to bilk the government, and don't even get him started on the ADA. He told me how they would have taken care of this problem in his old neighborhood in Boston, how it would only have taken a little while to make the undesirables feel unwanted enough to leave—no government necessary. He told me this was what he had moved to the country to get away from and complained about what this would do to real estate values and asked if this wasn't the zoning commission's responsibility to prevent. "I know you think I'm a redneck, Gary, but I'm not. I'm a Constitutionalist, and whatever people do in their own homes, I don't care," he said. "And I'm a Christian. I pray for these people every day. But the minute I see them sitting out on their porch and smoking their butts and watching our kids go by on the school bus…" He didn't finish his thought. I didn't tell him the house lacked a front porch, nor did I point out that you can't have it both ways—country life and city ways, hate the government but ask it to protect you. Instead, I thanked him for listening and he thanked me for calling and promised to talk to the people he already knew to be upset and tell them they could put down their guns—a promise whose apparent necessity canceled out its comfort.

Whatever Pete did or didn't tell his friends was not enough. Trips to the dump and the post office turned into marathons, with citizens collaring me to ask what was going on, and, even more, to tell me I was responsible for these deplorable developments. Why, they all wanted to know, had I not alerted the town to the fact that the sex offenders were coming? If only they'd known, they seemed to be saying, they could have organized and kept them out.

I stopped going out to the dump and the post office. I visited Perry Motors, but as I got to the front door of the garage, a woman flew out. She wanted to know what she could tell "my mothers"—evidently a group of younger women whom she was advising. "How could you let this happen?" she asked. I began my explanations. She cut me off. "I'll tell you what the problem is," she said, wagging a finger toward my face. "It's Pfizer. Do you know prisoners can get Viagra for free, paid for by the state?"

Scotland

I told her I didn't know that, waved a quick good-bye to Russell, and fled.

The meeting was my idea, although it did not take long for me to doubt its wisdom. I had thought that an opportunity for citizens to air their grievances directly to Reliance House officials, and to hear their response, might be oil on troubled waters. I thought if people heard that the town risked civil rights prosecution if it tried to prevent disabled people from living here, that even without Reliance House, sex offenders, convicted and otherwise, lived among us—mostly, unlike these men, neither disabled nor supervised—and that most sex offenses were perpetrated by family members or other people familiar with the victim, not by men who snatch children out of their backyards: I thought if they knew all this, they might turn their attention to measures they could take to make themselves feel less frightened.

But then in the two weeks leading up to the meeting, a woman named Wendy, who lived next door to the sex offenders and who seemed to be leading the group of concerned citizens, canceled the meeting she'd arranged with me, at which I had hoped to offer the face of a town government that understood how disturbing it was to have your sense of security suddenly threatened, and to provide her with my expertise in figuring out what could (and couldn't) be done. The next day, the first selectman told me that Wendy and her group were convinced that we were changing the definition of family to accommodate the sex offenders. A few days later, I ran into a man who informed me that he had determined that while Connecticut law banned firearms within a 500-yard radius of a home, it allowed you to carry a bow and arrow right to the property line. And I got an email relaying a message that had appeared on the group's Facebook page wondering whether they could carry their weapons to the meeting.

I couldn't back out, but I did call Reliance House. I told them this would be their meeting, that they would be seated alone at the front of the room, that I would give a quick introduction, sum up the events that led to their presence in town, remind everyone that what they were doing was protected by law, and suggest that they use this forum to get information that might reassure them. "Then," I said, "I'm throwing you to the wolves."

Scotland

So here we are, gathered in the grade school gym, to which the meeting has been moved because the firehouse hall can hold only two hundred people. By 7:00, nearly every one of the 350 seats is filled—more than twenty percent of the town, and closer to half of its registered voters. People are clustered together, talking excitedly. It might be a school play or a bake sale, although those aren't usually attended by a tall state police sergeant, his Smokey Bear hat pulled down close to his eyes.

I approach Wendy, whom I have still not met. She looks to be around 40. Her sandy kinky hair is pulled back in a tight knot that exaggerates her shiny skin and wide eyes. She is surrounded by four or five other women. I have emailed her a couple of times to tell her (after commending her for her efforts) that we might have to limit speakers to three minutes or so, but that she was welcome to make a single, long presentation on her group's behalf. She hasn't returned the emails. She's ignoring me now. I interrupt, introduce myself, shake her hand, and ask how much time she wants. "At least an hour," she says, pointing to a stack of papers, indexed with sticky notes and paper clips. She has brought a music stand to put them on.

I sweep my arm around the room. "There are more than 300 people here. We can't be here all night." She tells me they have brought sleeping bags and turns back to her huddle. "How about thirty minutes?" I ask. She shrugs.

I call the meeting to order. I thank everyone for coming. I tell them I understand why they are upset, and doubly so because they've been taken by surprise. I tell them I can see why they would be angry and disappointed with the zoning commission for not protecting them. I apologize for our inability to do that. I tell them what I knew and when I knew it and why I hadn't Paul Revered the news. I tell them about our problematic definition of family and the ADA, and I assure them that our attempt to redefine family is not an attempt to ex post facto the sex offenders into compliance but just a way to create a regulation that brings us into the 20th if not the 21st century.

They do not laugh at my little joke, just as their faces do not soften as I acknowledge their upset or nod in comprehension as I explain what has transpired to get us here. I feel pinned under the pitiless halogen lights, and I do not say the rest of what I have planned to say, about how even if we are not going to welcome them, it is our duty to find a way to live with sex offenders because they are in our midst, and not just the ones cared for by Reliance House. Instead, I turn the mic over to the six Reliance House people seated at the table. Let them stand up for sex offenders, I'm thinking. I move to the side of the room and sit down next to the state trooper.

The director, a bearded 70-year-old named Dave, talks quietly and earnestly about how much he understands the fear that has brought them there, and how he wishes to reassure them of Reliance House's intentions and integrity. He tells them that in their 30 years as an agency with 240 staff, never, not once, has someone run off from their care. He explains something I'd only found out a couple of days before: that the tenants were not disabled developmentally, but intellectually—what we used to call mentally retarded, with IQs less than 70, someone will explain later. In hindsight, Dave says, not having contacted the community earlier was a mistake, one for which he takes full responsibility and wishes to apologize. Then he turns the meeting over to the other staffers. They introduce themselves and describe their program and what life in the house is like. They explain that only two of the tenants are sex offenders, that the house is staffed by three aides all day, that whenever they venture out, each man has his own minder, and that in the night, there are two and sometimes only one staffer. They open the discussion.

I go back up front to ask the first question. I know the tenants have authorized Reliance House to release the details of their disabilities, I say. So what are the particulars? Dave and the staff are circumspect, evading the question until a man in the crowd shouts at me that I have not made them answer—more evidence, apparently, that I am on the wrong side. I go back to my seat by the cop.

Wendy stands up at her music stand. She introduces herself. She describes her family, her husband and three children, two of them young girls, and their horses and chickens and their love for the country life. She chokes up, pauses, takes a few deep breaths, and continues. "On April 17, a town resident knocked on my door and told me that three high-risk sex offenders had moved in next door. I was aghast. How could this have happened? Why didn't we know?" She explains that her husband went to Town Hall that night and found out that "town officials had just found out themselves." She looks up at me. "No one seemed to have any insight into this."

Wendy peppers the panelists with statistics about sex offenses, about disabilities, about the number of staff. She leafs through her papers and reads from scientific studies, from law books, from newspaper accounts. She asks the town lawyer for his expert opinion about intellectually disabled sex offenders. (He doesn't have one.) Then she turns to me. "*Doctor* Greenberg," she says, "what is your professional opinion about intellectually disabled people and sex offenses?" I follow the lawyer's lead.

After her half hour is up, others line up at the microphones. They cite statistics about recidivism. They wonder why the residents couldn't be housed elsewhere—perhaps in the abandoned "training school" that once housed mentally retarded adults just up the road, or in another such place down on the shoreline. They assert and reassert that they do not want sex offenders living among them, that there has to be a better place to put them. They suggest that the residents finagled their diagnoses in order to avoid responsibility and subvert the judicial system. They ask repeatedly about the alarm system at the house. If, "God forbid, [the residents] were out of the line of sight," a woman wonders, would the alarm system notify the staff? Would it go off if someone opened a window? They point out that Scotland has no local police and that state police, dispatched from barracks more than a half hour away, are notoriously slow to respond to calls for help. "That's why everybody out here has guns," one man says. And over and over again, they accuse Reliance House of "ruining" their town. "We don't want you here," a woman says, as if that were not plain.

The panelists respond in flat and measured tones. The institutional model is a thing of the past, they say. Sex offenders, once released from custody, are free citizens, and can and do live anywhere—forty of them, all but these three unsupervised, within a five-mile radius of the Reliance House home. Intellectual disability is a lifelong diagnosis, not something that one can claim only after a crime has been committed. As for the alarm, it is only on the doors, and was installed at the residents' request. The staffer refrains from adding that his

charges were more concerned about who might
break in to harm them than about being seized
by the sudden impulse to squeeze out a window
and molest a child. When someone asks why they
didn't just put "GPS tags" under the skin of the
residents, the woman from Reliance House only
says, "Because they are not animals."

Sitting again off to the side, sandwiched
between the first selectman and the state trooper,
I feel a little sorry for the panel, but mostly I am
relieved—not only to be out of the glare, but because
the questions have begun to take a turn I think is
favorable to me. Most of the speakers are women,
and many are speaking passionately, sometimes
tearfully, about the toll of sexual abuse, about their
fears for their daughters, about how the safety they
thought they'd achieved by moving to Scotland has
been shattered. "I don't see how you can sit there in
good conscience and look at us," one woman says,
her voice pinched with emotion, "and tell us that
our kids have to suffer this, that we can no longer
be a nice, safe town, that we just have to take this!"
Some women offer tearful and moving testimony
about being molested and assaulted. People,
especially the men in the audience, shift uneasily

in their seats as they disburden themselves. The first selectman leans over to tell me this was off the point.

But of course this is exactly the point. The panic is about sex and violence and the constant fear, whipped up by cheesy TV movies and sensationalist news channels and celebrity magazines and the inexhaustible human imagination, that predators lurk around every corner—a terror that can only be amplified by a sex offender registry that gives people no idea of what to do about the fact that the mug shot of their new neighbor is staring back at them from the computer screen. I'm thinking even this crowd of dedicated recriminators couldn't turn this into my fault. More to the point, sexually traumatized women are my professional bread and butter, the kind who feel comfortable around me, and to whom I know how to respond. I may have failed to alert them to the coming danger, I may think a house full of supervised disabled sex offenders is far from the most pressing hazard they face, I may wish they could find a more constructive way to manage their pain, but surely they have to know my sympathies are with them, that I know what it is like to be hurt and forever marked.

Scotland

The first selectman leans over again. "Gotta watch out for that blonde," he says, pointing to the next woman in line. "She's gonna have something to say to you." It takes me a second to make out her face. She's Barbara, a real estate agent—and his girlfriend. After remarking on the effect of sex offenders on neighboring real estate values, she demands that I return to the front of the room. "You represent the town residents," she says when I take my place. "You work for us. You're supposed to protect us and you chose to keep the information to yourself." The crowd bursts into applause.

A dark-haired woman named Diana, one of the few inquisitors whom I recognize, waves a paper at me. It is from my website, she says, and it claims that I treat people with sexual problems. This means I have a conflict of interest, she says, and I should disqualify myself. Then, as if it is just dawning on her that there was no decision to recuse myself from, she says that I should resign. Applause breaks out again.

One after another, the women now take the mics to decry my failure to speak up, my malfeasance, my dishonesty, their charges punctuated by loud cheering. Asked why I didn't know about the flaw in our definition of family, I explain that we don't have the resources to mount a wholesale revision of the regulations. "Well, I would like you to do that," she says. "That's what we pay you for." The audience claps, but she's only getting started. "Do you care about the people in Scotland? If you did, you wouldn't let this in your town." I look up at the ceiling (or maybe to heaven) to compose a response. "Don't roll your eyes!" she says. "Don't you know how disrespectful that is? I'll hold a mirror up to you—it's like you don't care at all." Others in the audience chime in. I'm not only disrespectful; I'm a disgrace. I shouldn't be rolling my eyes but hanging my head in shame. The applause rockets around the gym. I can't make out who is saying what, and it hardly matters. All I can see is the four or five women grouped together closely at the mic ten feet away, all shaking their heads and wagging their fingers at me, their hard eyes glaring. The only traumatized woman I can think of is Hester Prynne.

It's past ten, we've been at this for three hours, and I'm disheartened and more than a little scared. I can't think of anything to say, at least anything that won't get sucked up into the gathering cyclone and rain back down on me. I glance around the room looking for a single friendly face, and find Pete, already in line at the mic. We've decided to end the meeting at 11, sleeping bags or no. I count the remaining people in line. It looks like he'll get to speak before time is up. Maybe, I think, he'll speak up for me, will say that I'm really not such a bad guy, that I really wasn't rolling my eyes, that I have spent hours and days working to protect their property values and, as our master plan puts it, "the rural look and feel of Scotland." Maybe he will talk about our phone call, tell them how forthright and concerned I was, and, if he speaks near the end, maybe this will be what people carry home with them.

Pete does indeed talk about our phone call. I called, he says, to ask him to tell people to put away their pitchforks and torches. But then he recalls that I told him the men were severely retarded and supervised, one aide to a man, line-of-sight, 24/7. But, he explains, it turns out they are only mildly retarded and there is only one aide in the house overnight. "You lied to me, Gary, and I repeated those lies," he says. And that's not all. In recent days, he's been looking over the minutes of the recent zoning meetings, and "I was kinda stunned. I was disgusted. We trust our elected officials to make things better for our families," but we've been wasting time and lawyer money on redefining family in order to help "a business caring for criminals." Pete looks up at me. His eyes are bulging more than usual. He pauses for a moment. I can see he is rearing back for the knockout punch. "It is my opinion," he says, "that this is one of your social engineering experiments, Gary, and I think you should resign." The applause is loud and long.

As the lawyer tries to explain one more time that redefining family has nothing to do with Reliance House, I slink out of the hall. I walk past the town clerk and administrative assistant whom I took on years before. I think they are having sauce-for-the-gander thoughts; I don't blame them. I step outside to call my wife, who rang in the midst of Pete's denunciation, worried that something bad has happened to me. As I am assuring her that indeed it has, and still is, Pete walks out to have a smoke.

"I'm sorry," he says as I put my phone back in my pocket.

"Don't be. You meant it, right? The only thing

worse than calling me a liar in public would be if you didn't really mean to do it." I bum a cigarette. We stand out in the cool night air and smoke together. I don't remember what we talked about.

I go back inside in time to hear Wendy speak again, followed by the last speaker of the evening, Bud. He lives in a house just down the hill from Teeny Rood's old place. Rumor has it he has offered Reliance House what they had paid for the home, cash on the barrelhead, if they would just go away. He doesn't mention this. Instead, he talks about his psychology degree and his business degree and how he knows a house full of sex offenders is a bad thing. We adjourn the meeting. Bud comes right up to me, finger at my chest. "You have only one job now," he says. "Get rid of these people."

A few days after the meeting, I stopped by Guy's house. Over the years since I deposed him, I have seen him from time to time: at a local breakfast joint, where we spar jovially over who would pay for the meal; on the road, where I wave at him behind the tinted glass of his Lincoln Navigator; and at the post office, where once, on a bright summer day, I asked him how his television reception was, which made him smile. But I hadn't seen him in quite a while, maybe a year. I'd heard rumors that he was in poor health. I parked at the base of the cell tower and walk to the door. It took him a while to answer the bell. He was wearing a tracksuit. He'd let his hair go gray, and he was leaning on a cane. A television set played loudly in the background. He gestured me to a sofa on his enclosed porch. We made small talk, and then he asked me what he could do for me.

"I'm here to apologize," I said.

He looked puzzled. "For what?"

"For what I did to you. I had no idea what it was like to stand in front of a room full of people who hate you. I found out the other night, and I am really sorry for my part in that."

Guy waved his hand. "Oh, I enjoyed it!" he said. "And I was right. Carl was an asshole. No one wanted to believe me, but he was an asshole, and eventually everyone else figured that out." (Carl had finally quit, tired of being vilified.) We talked about the meeting, zoning man to zoning man. He'd heard about it, of course. He understood why I didn't say anything; he knew I didn't do anything wrong. He offered to "put the word out." Then he gave me a tour of his tidy ranch, which is the house he grew up in, and reminisced about his father and his uncle and his cousins. The walk-through winded him. He sat down heavily at his kitchen table, offered me a seat. I said I had to go, that my dog was in the hot car. I extended my hand, told him again I was sorry. As I turned to go, I had an impulse to hug him. Instead, I squeezed his meaty shoulder and left.

I have not gotten rid of the sex offenders. And the neighbors have not gotten rid of me, at least not yet. There is a petition circulating demanding my removal, and I'm not sure I will serve out my term on the zoning commission, which does not expire until 2017. I wish I could either fall on my sword or stay the course in order to uphold some great principle, that I could be either a tireless advocate or a martyr to some noble cause. But I'm not a zoning commissioner because I think zoning is a transcendent affair of state, or because I am committed to engineering a just society in which sex offenders play an integral role. I'm a zoning commissioner because I think participating in civic life is a good thing and because it makes me feel like I belong.

Or at least it used to. Now I'm not so sure. Last week, my son, who is sixteen, got a text message. "Your dad is a real dick," it said. Earlier in the day, before I knew about the text, I had run into the father of the girl who sent it, a guy I'd done business with in the past. He looked right through me. A couple of days ago, my wife asked a neighbor who is trying to sell his house if he was having any luck. "No," he said, "but maybe your husband would like to sell it to a sex offender." At the post office, people look away and hurry to their cars. The shunning isn't complete. A former first selectman called to tell me he'd heard I'd "gotten crucified," and that if he'd been there he would have stood up for me. I dropped in at Perry Motors, where I think I am still welcome, and Russell asked how my transformer was doing; the joke wasn't quite as funny as it once was, but it was at least friendly. I got an email from a woman expressing concern and sympathy. She warned me about the petition and offered to send a copy my way. I ran into another longtime resident in a store in a neighboring town. I thought I saw pity cross her face. "I had to leave at about 8:30," she said. "I was just too disgusted." She recalled the Klan rally.

"Why is it that when this town gets into the news, it's always about something negative?"

This morning, I met my Saturday breakfast friends—a truck driver, a farmer, and a mechanic—just before dawn. They were outraged to hear about the text message to my son. "You want to go after me, okay, but bring my kids into it, and I'll be up your ass in a heartbeat," the mechanic said as we rode toward the diner. That wasn't exactly how I saw it—I just felt bad that my son had to read the text—but I appreciated the support. They were sympathetic, but definitely not pitying. "You know, Greenie," the same guy said later, "this isn't really about the sex offenders. These people have probably disliked you all along. You just finally gave them a reason." He was kidding, I think, just as he was kidding later when he said he'd catch a ride back to his shop with the truck driver because he didn't want to be seen with me in the daylight.

The conversation turned to other topics: the difficulty of getting a decent front-end alignment, the young woman who had come to town to accuse a local citizen of fathering her out of wedlock, the man who was trying to build a road that was beyond his expertise and his equipment. "Everyone wants to be something they're not," said the farmer.

Indeed, I wanted to be part of something that I wasn't born into. I wanted to put on Scotland like a new skin. Which I did manage to do, but it turns out that Kipling was right: a skin that you can't shed can be itchy and uncomfortable, and the only thing worse than not being able to remove it is having it torn off. "It is always possible to bind together a considerable number of people in love, so long as there are other people left over to receive the manifestations of their aggressiveness," Sigmund Freud once wrote, adding that "in this respect, the Jewish people, scattered everywhere, have rendered most useful services to the civilizations of the countries that have been their hosts." But it wasn't anti-Semitism that brought me down (although I'm sure my background did not help). It's something much simpler, something that Hawthorne had figured out a century before Freud: no community, and especially no community as tight-knit as a New England village, exists without someone or something to hate. I moved to the country to get away from alienation and fragmentation, to acquire a home and a sense of belonging, to live in a place where people take care of one another, but I forgot what Shirley Jackson knew: that every community has its lottery, that a ticket is the price of admission, and someone has to lose.

After Wendy's final comments, she and her husband embraced in the aisle. The love between them was palpable, as was the love of all the people who spoke about their children and the dangers they faced. In the parking lot after the meeting, I heard people tell each other how glad they were to have met and gotten close, even if the circumstances were terrible. As angry as I was with them, as frightened and humiliated as they had made me feel, as much as I wished that their outrage was turned toward the truly outrageous and that their love was more expansive, I was also moved. Who could not be? Who is not distressed to discover that despite all the measures we can take or that can be taken on our behalf, we are still not safe, that life can still turn on a dime? Who is not terrified when danger steps up on the porch and knocks at the door? Who could not wish, as they wished, that our lives could be made safe, that we could circle up around a fire and feel warm and protected and impervious to harm?

Gary Greenberg

I used to think I would be buried near the Perrys and all the other Yankees who lived and died here, at the foot of the road to Teeny Rood's place. But that may not happen. I may not be able to stay in Scotland, and if I do, it may always be as one of the people left over. I regret this as deeply as I have ever regretted anything, but while I am resigned to it, I doubt I'll ever stop wishing that someone will welcome me back with a bowl of sourdough on my doorstep.

Epilogue

Four Months Later

Rumors, spread mostly by me, of my own demise have proved to be exaggerated. I'm still here. I've got my eye on a nice little plot in the cemetery. And while there are some people who might like to see me move into that little piece of real estate sooner rather than later, for now I am still the Chairman of the Planning and Zoning Commission of the Town of Scotland.

Not that this resolution came easily. In the first few weeks after my Hester Prynne moment, someone called the regional health district office to lodge a complaint about the septic system at the house, which she deemed insufficient for the fifteen staff people that the group insisted, against all the evidence, were living there. A state police prowl car parked in front of the house set off a flurry of phone calls to the first selectman, wondering whether one of the residents had escaped. (The police had logged it in as an "administrative visit.") Another email from me to Wendy, this one offering to discuss the re-definition of family, went unreturned. The Town Hall ladies were treating me with some mixture of pity and contempt. I let on to the first selectman's administrative assistant, the woman whose financial practices I had questioned when she was first selectman, that this was beginning to really bother me. "Been there. Done that," she said, and I thought I saw the satisfaction of revenge in her eyes.

A sympathetic woman emailed me a draft of the petition being circulated by the Truly Concerned Citizens of Scotland, as the group was now calling itself. "Inconsistencies in the dissemination of information from the only public official to have knowledge of the facility have caused extreme concern and panic within the community," it said. I had "made [my] career working in the Mental Health field," had written and published books, was "a licensed practicing psychotherapist and so, at the very least, there is the appearance of impropriety." Not only that, but I had failed to uphold the mission of the zoning commission set forth in the introduction to the zoning regulations— to preserve property values, promote the general welfare, and "secure safety from fire, PANIC, and other disasters." (The caps are not in the original.) And so I should resign—and not just me, but two other commissioners, both of whom the TCC had found guilty of spotty attendance at meetings, and one of whom, because he had received approval for a subdivision, was guilty of conflict of interest.

The TCC canvassed at the dump. They went door-to-door. They set up shop on the grade school grounds, with the approval of the principal. (She may have been unaware that allowing the TCC to advocate on public property opened the door to any other political group—the Ku Klux Klan, say, or maybe NAMBLA—that wanted the same access, or she may just have been sympathetic, or perhaps just afraid to say no to a group of enraged moms. I was in any event not in a position to point this out.) The TCC planned to present the petition at the next regular zoning meeting, three weeks after the initial one. I heard they were making t-shirts for the occasion. I wondered if the silkscreen would feature a man in the stocks.

I found myself thinking about Richard Nixon, Chris Christie, Rod Blagojevich, and all the other once successful public figures who had been found guilty in the court of public opinion long before any judicial proceedings—and guilty not of their crimes, but of something more fundamental: of being scoundrels. I wondered about the anatomy of downfall, how much these collapses were due to the material evidence—the tapes and emails, the money stashed in freezers, the wide stances and stained dresses—and how much the result of being scoured to the bone by a narrative wind. I mean, show me a person whose reputation can withstand the assault of a storyteller armed with animus and the Internet, and I'll show you a unicorn. And show me a person who can tolerate that treatment for very long, and I'll show you a politician, or at least someone with a belly that burns hotter than mine.

Not that there wasn't material evidence. I had not sounded the alarm, and of course I could have. I could have easily let the news slip at Town Hall or the post office and let gossip take its course; the resulting ugliness would at least not have been about my character. And I had presided over the redefinition of family; there was no question that I thought marriage and blood were inadequate criteria for determining who should be able to live together. You didn't have to be a Rove or a Goebbels to weave these facts into a story about my wish to socially engineer Scotland, especially not now, when narrative studies have escaped the academy, spin doctoring has become a national pastime, and Fox News has crowned every man a hermeneutical king. And you didn't have to be a coward to decide you didn't want to subject yourself any further to that treatment. I decided to resign.

But not quietly. Much as I am in favor of taking responsibility for my life, if for no other reason than the illusion it provides that fate is not really in charge, at some point being responsible means getting over yourself. Sometimes it means recognizing that other people are the problem. Sometimes, in other words, it means telling citizens, truly concerned or not, where the bear shits in the buckwheat.

That expression, by the way, is one of the best things I've learned from Russell Perry. I love its profanity and its alliteration and its strange juxtaposition of beast and grain. I'll bet you will find yourself saying it at least once in the next week or so. But don't squander it. It would be a shame to turn it into a cliché.

My opportunity to use it came at the first monthly meeting of the zoning board after our big night. It was held at the firehouse. About 80 people showed up, far fewer than the earlier meeting, but many more than usually attend. Some of them wore blue t-shirts that bore a crude map of Scotland over the words, "Truly Concerned Citizens of Scotland." The women who had jeered me sat together. Wendy's husband was with them. He never said a word.

Early in the meeting, I introduced a lawyer from the U.S. Attorney's office. His name was David Nelson, and he had come all the way from New Haven to talk to us about the Americans with Disabilities Act. It wasn't hard to persuade him to make the trek—he'd caught wind of the kerfuffle and was eager to head off any violations of civil rights, as well as to try to offer clarity and an outside perspective on the topic. With his Elliot Ness eyes and Jack Friday suit, Attorney Nelson looked every bit the part of a no-nonsense lawman—an impression his PowerPoint about the history of disability or his everyday stories about returning vets and service dogs in restaurants did little to soften.

Only a few slides in, the crowd rebelled. They didn't want to listen to some government lawyer go on about war heroes and handicap ramps. They wanted to talk about GPS chips and locked fences and bars on windows. They wanted to talk about the ruination of their town.

After a few citizens had gotten in their licks, Pete the farrier rose from his seat. "Welcome to Scotland," he said, a touch of droll in his voice. He reassured the attorney that the town had nothing against disabled people. But criminals—well, that was a different matter. People understand the difference between disability and criminality, he said, a point picked up by subsequent speakers. The problem, as one of them put it, was that the residents of Reliance House were "hiding underneath the label of disability." How was it possible that the town could not have a say about the criminals in its midst? Why didn't they have to prove that they were really disabled before they could move into the house?

"The President and Congress made a decision," he replied. "You can't make people continually prove their disability. It's the law," and if you don't like it, "you can write your congressman and tell him to change the law."

"But we're not discriminating against disability. We're discriminating based on their being criminals," the woman responded. Can't a town limit how many criminals can live together? Can't it require its criminals to place perimeter alarms on their houses? Can't it lock the gates around their houses?

"You want to lock them up again?" he asked. He sounded incredulous.

"We just want the town to be safe."

"If I understand you right, you're saying that certain segments of the population should be subject to scrutiny in the form of microchipping and locked perimeters," he responded, "even after they've done their time. By that logic, why not restrict everyone?"

"But if you have any experience at all with people in prison, you know that if you put a bunch of criminals together everyone knows what happens.

They get ideas from each other, they…"

"Ma'am," he said, "I am a Federal prosecutor. I understand what criminals are."

After nearly an hour, Assistant US Attorney Nelson was still only on his third slide. He had not managed to persuade the crowd that the government was here to help, and they had not convinced him to order up those fences and microchips. I cut off his presentation, with apologies, on the grounds that we had other business to attend to, and opened the hearing on our definition of family. I steeled myself, but the argument never materialized. Our proposal to decide how many dogs constituted a kennel generated more controversy than our attempt to decide how many people made a family.

I doubted the Truly Concerned Citizens had finally accepted the fact that we weren't trying to give back-door accommodation to criminals. More likely, I thought, they had noticed the contradiction between hating the government and asking it to enforce their notion of family. Or perhaps that they were keeping their powder dry for other matters, like their petition. And that was a battle in which I intended to take the first shot.

"Before we move on," I said, "I have something

to say."

I'd been thinking about my speech for a week or so, in the obsessive way you think about what you would have said to someone who mistreated you or someone you love. In the car, in the shower, taking a walk, it assembled itself. I never bothered writing it down but by the time of the meeting I knew just what I wanted to say. The speech was a real stemwinder, at least by modern standards—a good ten minutes or so of oratory. It had been a hard few weeks, I said. Some people's expectations that the government would keep them safe had been sorely disappointed, and they suddenly found themselves living in fear. For my part, I'd seen relationships cultivated over three decades disrupted and destroyed. I'd felt the strain and so had my family. I'd withstood their withering four-hour attack—at a meeting, I reminded them, that I had convened for their benefit and at which no one had stood up for me—without lashing out at them. I'd done that, I said, because I thought that having someone to blame would be helpful. I wasn't glad to have provided this service, but only in hopes that they would get it out of their system and move on.

But then, I told them, I heard about the petition,

and that it wasn't just me they were after, but two other commissioners, men who had collectively served for 45 years. "Where are you going to stop?" I asked. "At long last, have you left no sense of decency?" I wanted to say, but did not—although on the tape I can hear the words on the tip of my tongue.

"I would love the opportunity to defend myself," I said. "I'd love the opportunity to hear how it's a conflict of interest that I work in the mental health field and write books, and that I then went on to make no decision about Reliance House. But I'm not going to do that." I reminded them that conflict of interest is a serious charge, an accusation that carries legal weight. "Maybe you didn't think this through," I said, but the town would have to pay for my defense. "And that would be wrong"

And then to the point. "I didn't sign on to the zoning board because I have some love for zoning. I'm a hippie-libertarian at heart. I signed on because I wanted to help out. That's all. And if I can't do that, if in fact I am hurting the town, if I've become a polarizing figure who is going to cost us money to defend against charges that are frankly ridiculous, then I am not going to do that. So I will resign as you have asked."

All this was prepared. What wasn't prepared, and what I was not prepared for, was the way my voice broke when I got to this part. I'd been too busy feeling relieved and vengeful to recognize how sorry I was to be doing this, and how little choice I felt I had. I just didn't have whatever those downfalling politicians had that allowed them to persist until the last jury rendered the last verdict, and I realized just how disappointed I was in myself about this, how limited the satisfactions of passive aggression, how much I would miss watching the cavalcade of citizens marching through with their beefs and their dreams, how much I enjoyed presiding over this well-meaning if doomed attempt to negotiate the terms of living together. And although I had come into the meeting fully prepared to quit, and at least partly relieved at the prospect, I suddenly found myself wavering, and then off-message entirely.

"The only condition, the only way I can not do this, is if that petition disappears," I said. "Either it goes away by the end of the day tomorrow, or I do."

I probably should have stopped there, but really, how many bear-in-the-buckwheat moments does life offer you? So I threw in a few extras. I told them I commended what they had done, even if I didn't commend them for how they treated me. And then I told them the story of Guy and me, including the part about apologizing to him—"because I was ashamed," I said—and explained that this is how I got to be the chair of the zoning commission. "My point is, this is going to happen again," I said. "It's in the nature of the people in small towns to turn on one another, and it seems to be increasingly in the nature of our entire country. And the next time it does, please have some humanity. Don't make the mistake I made with Guy. Remember that the person you are tearing to pieces is a human being who wants the same thing you do—a beautiful town in which to live.

"And that's all I have to say."

The room was silent. But then the first selectman stood to speak. He said that he didn't want me to resign. He told me he thought I had done a good job as chair of the zoning board. So did a farmer. And a couple of members of the board. And our zoning agent. And even Russell Perry, who attends all our meetings but rarely speaks in public. He told a little story about how he'd been one of the first zoning board members, and how hard it had been to do the job. It would be a great loss to the town if I resigned, they all were saying. They didn't exactly beg, but it was clear that something had shifted, at least enough for some people to risk being on my side and to let me know I mattered to them.

Which I have to admit was deeply gratifying, in exactly the way it would be in a movie, when, say, the Pale Rider finally sets things straight in the lawless town. Only I didn't have to wear a leather coat or learn to ride a horse or draw any weapons except words.

When Wendy said that she wasn't sure she could get the petition rescinded, that this wasn't her decision to make, I was pretty sure that she could, and it was, and she would—and the next day she did. But I already knew the tide had turned. I knew it as soon as Pete strode back into the room. He'd missed my performance while having a smoke and a chat with a former first selectman, but he picked up where he'd left off. "I've been reading your minutes," he said, "and I'm just disgusted. This is the analogy I'm going to use. You seem like the guys at the Moose Lodge. You agreed on this, you agreed on that, you agreed on who's bringing the sauce for the spaghetti dinner, on who's bringing the meatballs. Are we going to have meatballs or sausage?" Three weeks ago, or just a half hour ago, these would have been excellent laugh lines. But now he was greeted with silence, and an uncomfortable one at that. "Huh," he said. "It sure feels different in here."

After the meeting, people came over to me to shake my hand. Yankees to the last, they said very little, but it was there in the smiles, in the nods, in the way one woman—a woman who had been in the forefront of the attack—held onto my hand for just a moment longer than a handshake really takes. It was as if they were congratulating me, but mostly I think they were thanking me for finally defending myself. I had put out a fire that, much as it might once have warmed them, had gotten out of control. And for regaining some of my dignity. An individual's dignity belongs to the community too, and to insist on it is not only to spare everyone the pain of cringing for someone else, but also to make everyone a little stronger.

So for now anyway, I'm still the Chairman of the Planning and Zoning Commission of the Town of Scotland, County of Windham, State of Connecticut. Some things are different. Wendy, leader of the Truly Concerned Citizens, is now the clerk of the zoning board; we had an opening and she was the only one to apply. I think she wants to keep an eye on us. So does Pete, who continues to come to our meetings, presumably to make sure we weren't just talking about spaghetti. The fire has not gone out completely. At a recent meeting a commissioner brought up the subject of regulating where sex offenders can live, and the air was suddenly thick. But calm prevailed, and we moved on to the question of how many horses makes a commercial riding stable. The surface comity, the kind that is neither deep nor dangerous, had been restored.

Recently, the farmer I have Saturday breakfast with told me he had had a conversation with the first selectman. They'd been talking about the way the fight over Reliance House was a battle between "old Scotland" and "new Scotland," and how old Scotland had prevailed. I wasn't so sure they were right about that, but even if they were, and even if I was gratified to be granted membership in the old-timers' club, I was pretty certain that the victory, if that's what it was, was only temporary. No matter what measures we take, no matter how concerned the citizens, new houses will be built and new gravestones laid, new worries will chatter in our heads, new beliefs will take hold, and new people will move to town and, sooner or later, they (or their offspring) will become old-timers. And new occasions will arise to blame on someone, anyone, the passage of time, the way its fingers claw away the familiar, unravel it, and toss it to the wind.

Abut the Author

Gary Greenberg is the Chairman of the Planning and Zoning Commission of the Town of Scotland, Connecticut. He is also the author of four books, including The Book of Woe: The DSM and the Unmaking of Psychiatry and Manufacturing Depression: The Secret History of a Modern Disease. His features and essays have appeared in many publications, including The New York Times, The New Yorker, Rolling Stone, and Harper's, where he is a contributing editor. He is the recipient of the Erik Erikson Institute Prize for Excellence in Mental Health Media. A practicing psychotherapist, he lives with his family in Connecticut.

Made in the USA
Middletown, DE
22 December 2016